M000201613

The Orvis Shooting School
Method of
Wingshooting

The Orvis Field Guide Series

The Orvis Shooting School Method of
Wingshooting

Incorporating Firearms Safety

As taught at the shooting grounds at
ORVIS SANDANONA,
ORVIS MANCHESTER & ORVIS MAYS POND

*Text, Photographs and Illustrations
by Laurie Morrow, Series Editor*

WILLOW CREEK PRESS
MINOCQUA, WISCONSIN

Special thanks to Lars Jacob, Tom Deck and Peggy Long for their valuable assistance, Dan O'Connor for his time and dedication to this guide, and Tom Rosenbauer, without whom the *Orvis Field Guides* would not be possible.

Published by Willow Creek Press, PO Box 147, Minocqua, WI 54548

For information on other Willow Creek Press titles,
call 1-800-850-WILD

Library of Congress Cataloging-in-Publication Data

Morrow, Laurie.
The Orvis Shooting School method of wingshooting : incorporating firearms
safety, as taught at the shooting grounds at Orvis Sandanona, Orvis
Manchester & Orvis Mays Pond / text, photographs, and illustrations by
Laurie Morrow.
p. cm. -- (The Orvis field guide series)
ISBN 1-57223-314-1 (hardcover : alk. paper)
1. Shotguns. 2. Upland game bird shooting. I. Orvis Shooting School. II.
Title. III. Series.
SK274.5 .M67 2000
799.2'028'34--dc21
00-009376

Printed in Canada

CONTENTS

PREFACE

THE ORVIS SHOOTING SCHOOL was founded in 1973 in response to a resurgence of interest in sport shooting not seen since the years between the world wars, when legendary American gunmakers such as Parker, Browning, Ithaca, and L.C. Smith produced among the first—and some of the finest—smokeless powder, fluid steel barreled shotguns to satisfy a burgeoning outdoor market. New England—now as then—is the traditional home of wingshooting in America. Here every fall, wingshooters pursue the stealthy grouse and the transient woodcock. It's a singular time of falling leaves and fallen apples, keen gun dogs, good guns and golden days. That Orvis established a shooting school in its own backyard in Manchester, Vermont, one of New England's most celebrated and picturesque towns, was only natural for a company dedicated to outdoorsmen and women, and the sporting way of life. Since then, the shooting grounds at Orvis Sandanona in Millbrook, New York, and Orvis Mays Pond near Tallahassee, Florida, have expanded and strengthened our commitment to shotgun sports.

If you can point, you can develop the skill to shoot. However, in order to progress, you must learn proper technique. The Orvis Shooting Method was developed specifically for the American upland gunner. If you are new to the sport, our method will teach you the principles of field-shotgunning. If you are a seasoned wingshooter, it will help you become a more consistent and reliable shooter. The techniques we teach are based on the principles developed by Englishman Robert Churchill early in the last century. Churchill maintained that a person not only has the ability to point, but the natural ability to point with remarkable accuracy. He applied this simple premise to wingshooting in his country. We have adapted it to wingshooting in ours.

For the purpose of this guide, we discuss upland bird hunting with double guns—that is, shooting a side-by-side or over/under. Not only are these the classic configurations for field guns, but we feel they lend themselves more appropriately to the sport.

The information in this guide will teach you the basic elements of wingshooting—proper gun fit, correct footwork, the ready position and visual concentration. These are the tools you will need to handle the many unpredictable situations found in the field, and, with practice, will prepare you for a lifetime of enjoyment as a skilled wingshooter.

—DAN O'CONNOR, Director
The Orvis Schools

INTRODUCTION

A WINGSHOOTER DOES NOT reach the pinnacle of his proficiency in his twenties or even thirties, the age men and women generally peak physically when it comes to most sports. Like a fine wine, a fine wingshooter improves with age. How he or she shoulders his shotgun becomes instinctive. It becomes habit, how he listens for the *whirr* of a whirling woodcock or the *whoosh* of a rocketing grouse through the cacophony of rustling autumn leaves. He's sure a pa'tridge will burst forth from a favorite secret covert on opening day (a day as sacred to a wingshooter as Christmas is to a Christian) and most opening days, one does. His setter will tremble on point, her muscles aquiver like rolling waves rippling on the sand. He'll take the bird with his second barrel because still, after all these years, a charging grouse on this most-anticipated of days takes him unawares. And when, at the end of that long and precious day, he returns home with the weight of that single solitary bird in his game bag, he is content. It is enough. The bird, after all, is merely a fraction of the wingshooting equation.

So, the years unfurl like the petals of a rose and through the passing seasons the wingshooter's memories acquire a golden glow that warms his old age. He has hung up his well-worn hunting coat on the peg. "Old Reliable" honorably decorates the wall, its last shot spent, the stock finish a warm and worn patina burnished by the years. His white-muzzled bird dog is curled in front of the crackling fireplace, woofing in her sleep. The old hunter shuffles quietly by, settles his stiff bones in his favorite chair and drifts off, dreaming of whistling woodcock and ricocheting grouse.

And he basks in the memories of days afield, when the birds flew fast, the gun shot true, and his dog's retrieves were bold and cocksure. If you were to ask the old wingshooter when it was that he reached the peak of his shooting form, he would say, with a grin, that he was in top form all of those years—with every bird taken and every bird missed. For there is no prime age for a wingshooter, only prime times.

* * *

The purpose of the *Orvis Shooting School Method of Wingshooting* is to help you develop the skills and qualities you need to become a first-class wingshooter. Whether it is upland birds, lowland birds, or birds of a different feather (that is, clay pigeons) the techniques that are taught at the Orvis Shooting School and illustrated in this handy guide will teach you to sight a bird and effect a clean kill consistently and effectively. This book will help you achieve a good and proper beginning, right from the start.

If you are a young, first-time shooter, these techniques will become the foundation upon which you can continually build through the years and bird seasons ahead. Every shot you fire, every shooting situation you find yourself in, will only serve to further your improvement and help you gain the proficiency you need to be a finished wingshooter.

If you are a relatively new shotgunner, the power to concentrate and rapid hand-eye coordination are the two principle skills that the Orvis Shooting Method can help you develop. It does not matter if you can no longer run a mile in less than ten minutes, or can score a field goal or a home run (though most certainly, it is to your great benefit to stay in shape). If, though, you already are a consummate and capable wingshooter, this book will surely serve as a valuable reference guide that can help you keep your shooting skills in check.

Whether you are beginning or continuing your journey as an upland gunner, never loose sight of the unspoken sportsman's creed — honor Nature and the birds she has provided. To do that, you need to know about the wildfowl you hunt. Learn about their life cycles and habitats. Respect for and knowledge of wildlife is essential to being a responsible hunter.

Being an effective shooter is also fundamental to responsible hunting. However, learning proper shotgunning technique alone will not make you a good wingshooter. As you strive to become a better shot, remember that it's time spent afield that will sharpen your skills. The mature wingshooter possesses a deportment garnered over a myriad of seasons, honed over countless flushes and flights, and scored by incalculable shots.

So, whether you are about to embark upon—or continue—your path as a wingshooter, remember this: Your best shot is yet to come.

—LAURIE MORROW, *Series Editor*
The Orvis Field Guides
Freedom, New Hampshire

WHAT IS THE ORVIS METHOD OF WINGSHOOTING?

THE ORVIS METHOD OF WINGSHOOTING is pretty fundamental: Combine concentration with proper form and technique and your shot can successfully contact the bird. Sounds simple, right? *Wrong*.

In theory, proper shotgun technique is easy to understand. In practice, it is an acquired skill that results from visual, physical, and mental conditioning. Shooting is a precision sport and, as with any sport, it requires time and training to do it well.

Our goal is to enable a person to shoot consistently well in just about any bird-hunting situation.

We didn't reinvent the wheel, but we did adapt England's Churchill school of shooting to fit the American wingshooter in his own hunting environment.

We literally begin from the ground up—with *footwork*. Proper footwork allows the shooter to move with the target, mount the gun, and swing in one free-flowing motion. A common problem among shooters, both new and seasoned, is separation of movement. This means the shooter will mount the gun before moving the body. It is impossible to maintain focus and keep up with the target if you mount the gun first and *then* attempt to swing to the target. *At no point should the bird beat the muzzle.* You must swing to the target as you mount the gun—do not mount and then swing. *Swing as you mount the gun.* That's the foundation of the Orvis method—and that foundation is built on proper footwork.

Many people who come to our schools are self-taught and have mixed priorities. Most people put the priority on the trigger hand, which hurries the gun mount before tracking the target. The priority in the Orvis method is the *forehand*. Wingshooting is a pointing game. The gun is an extension of the pointing hand, or forehand. The forend of the gun rests in the forehand, which initiates the gun. Yes, simple to understand. . . but no easy feat.

Many of our students are seasoned wing-shooters who come to the Orvis Shooting School because they have hit a plateau and don't understand why they can't shoot better. There is a flaw somewhere in the shooter's technique that inhibits his swing or gun mount and therefore causes him to shoot inconsistently. Orvis instructors detect the flaw and work with the shooter to correct it. For example, a slight drop of the shoulder will cause a misalignment. The accepted rule of thumb is that the distance between the muzzle of the gun and the pupil of the eye is 36 inches. If the barrel alignment (or line of sight) is off by $1/16$ inch, then the shot will be off one foot at 16 yards.

Oftentimes an experienced shooter presumes we can analyze his technique in one afternoon. There is no such thing as a "quick fix" when it comes to correcting improper technique. Chances are, the shooter will spend two or more days at the school so we can help him break down bad habits and create good habits. It is more difficult to re-train the muscle memory of an experienced shooter in order to "unlearn" incorrect technique than it is to mold a new shooter to shoot properly from the very beginning.

It's true that practice makes perfect, but if you are practicing the wrong form, you will only further exacerbate your problems. Self-analysis in such a situation is impractical. As in any sport, you need a good coach. Your coach at the Orvis Shooting School is a trained instructor and experienced wing-shooter who will help you eliminate problems such as misalignments, and work with you to perfect your technique so you can concentrate on making effective shots.

And that's the bottom line. The Orvis method of wingshooting is designed to help you shoot effectively and consistently in just about any field situation. Make the commitment to be a better wingshooter and we'll show you how.

GUN FIT

WHAT IS GUN FIT? Proper gun fit would be better described as gun*stock* fit. Correct gun fit is achieved when a gunstock is tailored to the individual so the barrel alignment and line of sight are the same. A properly fitted gun benefits the shooter in two ways. First, it allows the shooter to focus his full concentration on the bird. Second, there is less felt recoil. When a gun fits properly, it shoots where you are looking. Where you are looking and the point of impact must be the same if you are to hit the target accurately. That is where technique comes in. To shoot well, a gun must fit well. You should be certain that your gun fits you properly before you pull a trigger in the shooting field.

Most upland birds are effectively shot at 25-yards or less. In all likelihood, you should be able to hit a target at such close distance, right? Not so if the target is a winged rocket known as a grouse. Even the most seasoned wingshooter will attest that putting a bead on that feathered missile as it weaves through a copse of pines is one of the most challenging—and rewarding—reasons why he is an upland hunter.

A shotgun moves with a moving target. Gun fit is more crucial in wingshooting than in any other shooting discipline. It can make the difference between a clean kill and a sheer miss. This is due to several factors. First, there is little control over the shots presented in bird-hunting situations. Until the bird rises, you are never certain where it is coming from or where it is going. Second, the time you have to get into the ready position, mount the gun, and pull the trigger can be measured in seconds. During this brief time, you have to observe the speed and flight path of the bird in order to determine your shot. A shotgun is an extenuation of the shooter's sight line and hands. When the gun fits the shooter naturally, he should be able to focus on the target and not on the gun. If he has to think about the gun, he will lose concentration on the target. In wingshooting, failure to concentrate on the target invariably results in a missed shot.

A properly fitted gun will feel as natural to the shooter as if it were an extenuation of his own hands. He has a reliable sight line down the rib of the barrels that enables him to track the target effectively. *That's* the secret of successful wingshooting — focus on your target, never on the gun. If a gun fits well, you have no reason to look at the gun, jostle it into position, or wonder where the barrels are pointing. When a gun fits you, you will cheek the gun naturally as you point, follow, and swing through the moving target.

A properly fitted gun will allow you to point and focus on the bird. Anything that diverts your visual concentration on the bird will diminish your chance at an effective shot.

Gun to cheek, shoulder to gun

When a shotgun is mounted correctly, the appearance is one seemingly effortless motion. The butt of the stock settles snugly into the soft part of the shoulder. The shooter's head remains high and steady as the stock comes up and touches his cheek. The trigger is pulled and the cartridge is discharged.

The Elements of Gun Fit

When we refer to gun fit, we really mean how the gunstock fits the shooter. The gunstock is the most important element of shotgun fit. When the stock fits properly, the gun is working for and with you.

Noted 19th century British gunmaker and inventor W.W. Greener maintained that a gun tailored to the build of an average man will fit eighty percent of all shooting sportsmen. A common comparison is an "off the rack" suit of clothes. Chances are the suit will fit you, but a nip here and a tuck there will make it fit even better. The same theory applies to gunstock fit. What seems to be an imperceptible measurement (such as ⅛ inch shaved off or added to a comb) can have a dramatic effect on the point of impact.

How to check if your gun fits you properly

Even if you are of average build, gun fit is very individual. No two people are alike. Neck and arm length, shoulder slope, and facial structure are some of the factors that determine gun fit. (Contrary to popular belief, however, arm length is the least important factor.) You can get an idea of whether your gun fits you properly by performing the following exercise. Although not perfectly accurate, it can give you an idea.

Stand a safe distance back from a full-length mirror. Bring the gun up to your cheek and point at your right eye (if you are left-handed, point at your left eye). Hold this position. If the gun fits, you will see the pupil of your eye peeking over the rib. The rib will have the appearance of being ⅛ inch long, more or less. To be exact, the rib should

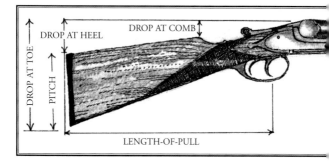

be cutting the bottom third of your pupil. If so, you will shoot 60/40, which means 60-percent of your pattern will be on top of the target and 40-percent will be below, or on the bottom, of the target. A gun that you shoot 60/40 or 70/30 is favorable for the rising shots encountered in upland hunting. If the pupil is cut in half, you are shooting the gun dead-on at 50/50, or fifty-percent above the target and fifty-percent below. This is desirable for pass shooting. If you see no rib

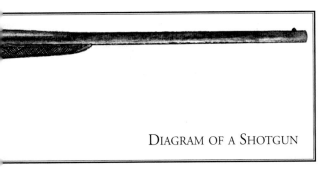

DIAGRAM OF A SHOTGUN

or, quite the opposite, too much rib, then schedule an appointment with a qualified shotgun fitter. He will measure you and adjust the stock so the gun will fit you properly.

We frequently hear someone say, "I've got ten guns and I only shoot one well." Likely as not, that one gun is the only one that fits him properly. We also hear seasoned wingshooters say, "My gun isn't shooting as well as it used to." Chances are there is a glitch in that person's technique; however, a fluctuation in a person's weight can also make a difference. Your shotgun fitter can solve the problem. Be aware, however, that adjustments made to a gunstock by a professional gunsmith who specializes in shotgun fit may be expensive. The gun has to warrant the expense. A factory or older gun may not justify it. Be sure to get an estimate of the work first. If you are restocking a gun, the condition and worthiness of the action and barrels must deserve a new stock. Restocking a gun, even with a plain, semi-inletted blank of American walnut, can run in excess of $2,500. A custom stock in deluxe Turkish walnut will cost in the multiple thousands of dollars. It is not uncommon to pay upwards of $3,000 just for a nicely veined blank—and that's before the stock-maker even takes out a chisel. A 4X or exhibition

grade custom stock is the Mercedes of gunstocks—
and can cost about as a much.

It is certainly not necessary to restock a gun to
get a gun to fit. A professional gun fitter knows the
tricks of the trade to adjust a stock to fit you properly. Don't attempt to adjust a stock yourself.
Many shooters do not realize that when a stock is
shortened or lengthened, other dimensions of the
stock may need to be adjusted as well. Attempting
to add a recoil pad or sand off the butt will only
aggravate the problem. Stock fitting is a significant
and skilled professional undertaking that should
not be assumed by untrained hands.

Length-of-pull

Though we have stated that the length of a shooter's
arm is not the most important measurement in

proper gun fit, length-of-pull is the first measurement that a gun fitter must establish. From this, all else follows. The initial measurement for length-of-pull can change at any time during the gun fitting process.

Length-of-pull is measured from the center of the front trigger to the center of the buttstock. It is established by the length of the shooter's arm; however, it is also determined by the length of the neck, slope of the shooter's shoulder, and his facial structure. Although the standard for an American-made factory gun is approximately 14½ inches, many men and some women can take a longer stock to better advantage. Fifteen and one-half inches is not unusual for a long-limbed person. A professional gun fitter or stockmaker can install a buttpad or an extension to lengthen a stock. If a stock is too long, the stock can be cut or a buttpad can be replaced with a buttplate. Because the overall proportions of the gun must be factored into any stock alteration, especially cast, do not surrender your gun to a gunsmith who is willing to cut the stock or slap on a pad without fitting the gun to you first. Not every person who calls himself a gunsmith is a qualified gun fitter. In point of fact, there are amazingly few.

Gun fit also depends on the actual configuration of the gun. Most people shoot a side-by-side longer than they would an over/under because there is a tendency to shoot more cast in a gun whose barrels lie alongside one another, providing a wider sight plane.

When a gun fits properly, it will feel like the weight of the gun is equally distributed between both of your hands. A stock that is too long will force the shooter's forehand to slide back towards the hinge pin, creating a "muzzle flip," or seesaw motion when the gun is mounted. It will also put the butt of the stock low on the shoulder, forcing the shot to go high. A stock that is too short for a shooter makes the gun feel "whippy," which means it is difficult to maintain a flat, level swing and consistent mount. A gunstock that is too long or too short for the shooter has the same result: the gun won't feel right and will prevent the shooter from pointing the target properly.

When a stock is too short, the shooter runs the risk of feeling excessive recoil in the hand, nose or cheek. When the stock is too long, the gun becomes difficult to mount to the shoulder. Either way, shooting the gun can be uncomfortable—and when a gun is uncomfortable, the shooter will consciously or unconsciously anticipate discomfort, flinch and miss the target.

Drop at heel

Drop at heel is the distance from the plane of the rib, or "sighting plane," to the heel of the buttstock. Average drop is 2 to 2½ inches at the heel. Drop at heel is for comfort. This measurement aligns the butt of the gun to the proper place in the shoulder. Like length-of-pull, drop at heel is related to length of neck, slope of shoulders, and length of the arm. The measurement is taken from the shooter's earlobe to the top of his shoulder. The best way to adjust drop is to have a professional gunsmith bend the stock to fit you properly.

Drop at comb

Drop at comb is the stock measurement that adjusts the pupil properly over the eye. The elevation of your shot is determined by adjusting the drop at comb. Drop at comb is the distance from the rib to the comb. The average drop at comb is 1¼ to 1¾ inches. If there is too much, the shooter will stare at the back of the action instead of down the barrels. This will cause the gun to shoot low. Conversely, a gun with too little drop at comb will shoot high.

Pitch

Pitch is a result of the angle of the butt in relation to the rib. The purpose of pitch is comfort and regulation. The slope of the chest of the shooter is a factor in determining proper pitch. When the pitch is correct, the entire butt of the gunstock will equally contact the shoulder on its entire surface. This markedly reduces felt recoil and keeps the gun stable. If the gun has too much contact at the toe (not enough positive pitch), the gun will jump down because the recoil is being absorbed by the toe of the gun. For women shooters, shortening the toe is one way to reduce felt recoil. On the other hand, if there is too much positive pitch, the gun will jump up and there will be an increase in felt recoil. Pitch varies with the gun, the shooter, and the game bird. Upland bird hunters generally want a gun with a down-pitch of about 2 to 3 inches, since most shots are taken at relatively close range.

The duck hunter usually shoots his waterfowl gun with a shorter length-of-pull and more of a positive pitch than he would an upland gun due to the shooting positions he assumes in pass shooting and the extra padding that tends to result from wearing heavier clothing. If the shooter uses the same gun for upland and lowland birds, he will have to adjust his mount to correspond with the hunting situation.

A popular way to measure pitch is to place the butt of the gun flat on the floor with the receiver touching the wall; however, this is not an accurate method. Barrel length is a variable. If the gun has 26-inch barrels, the measurement is taken at the muzzle. If the gun has 28-inch barrels, the measurement is taken two inches below the muzzle. If the gun is not perfectly plumb to the floor, the measurement will be inaccurate.

At Orvis, our gun fitters determine pitch by measuring the angle of the buttstock in relation to the plane of the barrels in degrees. Barrel length is not a factor in this method of measurement. The most common pitch is +4 degrees, which is equal to 2 inches of downpitch. This will feel "right" to most wingshooters in most hunting situations. If the gun is intended for driven birds or trap, the stock will have less pitch.

Cast

Drop corrects elevation. *Cast* corrects windage, or whether you are shooting to the left or right of the target. A person needs cast at the face and at the toe. Cast at the face is related to facial structure—specifically, the width of the face in relationship to eye set. Cast at the toe relates to the natural pocket in the shoulder and the way it is canted. Average cast measurements are ¼ inch at the heel and ⅜ inch at the toe, more or less, depending on the shooter. The correct cast for a woman can make a significant difference in the way her gun fits. Usually a woman benefits from a little more cast at the toe than does a man. This enables her to look down the rib so that when she fires the gun, she will not flinch as a result of the discomfort of felt recoil along the side of her chest.

Also critical to gun fit is the thickness of the comb. In the case of a right-handed shooter, if the comb is too thick, the gun will tend to shoot to the left. If it is too thin, the gun may have a tendency to shoot to the right.

The term *cast-off* refers to a right-handed shooter; *cast-on* to a left-handed shooter.

Bending the stock

Most wooden gunstocks can be altered to the proper cast or drop by bending the stock at the grip one of two ways: "passively," or with steam. Both methods are professional gunsmith operations. Not every gunstock, however, is a candidate for bending. If the grain does not flow through the grip, the stock runs the risk of breaking at the wrist—a costly and difficult repair.

The Grip

The traditional game gun sports a straight stock (a.k.a. straight-hand stock or English grip). Less common is a type of semi-pistol grip known as the *Prince of Wales* stock. In a double-trigger, side-by-side shotgun, a straight stock is an advantage because it allows the trigger hand to move easily from the front trigger to the back trigger. A straight stock also keeps the hands and eyes in alignment with the barrels. A straight stock somewhat reduces the weight of the gun, which is desirable in a true light upland gun.

A pistol grip has benefits, too. It tends to relax the wrist position. Some shooters prefer a pistol-grip because it keeps the hand in place and gives a feeling of control over the gun. Many sporting clays shooters favor a pistol grip because it gives the gun lifting power.

The Forend

The forend is the handrest for the pointing, or lead, hand. Mechanically, its function is to hold the barrels of a gun on the frame, help cock the hammers, and operate the ejector mechanism. The traditional forend that is exclusive to side-by-side upland guns is the splinter forend (or forearm). A splinter forend is a thin, slender wooden forestock that is designed to fit comfortably into the palm of the lead hand and allows the shooter to swing the gun freely. When the barrels become hot from continuous firing, a splinter does little to protect the hand. Wearing shooting gloves or a removable leather forend that slides over the barrels are good solutions to prevent discomfort.

Beavertail and semi-beavertail (or "field") forends are more substantial in design than the splinter. These reduce the recoil effect slightly by giving the forward hand a more substantial gripping surface. Beavertail or field forends are standard on over/under guns and do well to protect the hand from hot barrels.

Barrel length

Two things determine barrel length: length-of-pull and type of shooting. As we have mentioned, longer barrels are desirable for pass shooting while shorter barrels are more appropriate for quick-point shooting. Also, barrel length should mate to the length of the stock. There is a misconception that the length of the barrels affects the weight of the gun. Barrel length affects the *balance* of a gun, but the difference, say, between 27- and 28-inch barrels does not significantly influence its weight.

The traditional straight grip, side-by-side shotgun in 12- or 16-gauge with 27- to 29-inch barrels is still considered the most versatile, desirable and popular configuration for an upland gun. The longer length barrels allows a more realistic lead perception. The increase in kinetic energy makes it harder to stop the gun, thereby sustaining swing.

The Top-rib

The top-rib of a gun has a decided effect on shooting. As we've discussed, when the shooter brings the gun to his cheek, the rib becomes an extension of his sight plane. There are four types of ribs used on double-barrel upland guns: *hollow*, *flat*, *swamped* and *straight*. Most side-by-side shotguns have *hollow ribs*. This type of rib is grooved and follows the outer curvature of the barrels. The lightest is the *swamped rib*, which dips to its lowest point halfway between the breech and muzzle. A *flat rib* gives the appearance of being squared as you look down the sighting plane. A *straight rib* is a true plane that is level at every point along its length. All ribs taper slightly from breech to muzzle in proportion with the outside edge of the barrels.

Balance

Balance, or *handling quality*, plays an integral part in how a gun points and swings. Proper balance is achieved when the form, dimensions, and distribution of weight of the gun are in proper relation to the shooter. The hinge pin is very close to the balance point on most double guns. If the weight of the gun lies forward of the hinge pin, the gun is barrel-heavy. If it is behind, the gun is muzzle-light. Waterfowl guns generally balance further forward to conform to pass-shooting.

FOOTWORK

A proper fitting gun is enhanced with proper technique. Lack of technique is the number one reason for missed shots. In this section, we will examine the elements of proper footwork, which is the foundation of effective technique.

PROPER FOOTWORK is the first critical element of effective wingshooting. A shooter's feet should maintain the center-point of gravity. When your feet are properly placed, you can pivot while keeping your shoulders square with the target. To do this, keep your feet as close together as possible without up-setting your balance. The feet should stay within the breadth of your shoulders. The degree of separation of the feet is related to shoulder width.

The wingshooter cannot always predict from which way the bird is coming. Proper stance allows the shooter to adjust to the flight path of the bird in almost any hunting situation. A right-handed shooter puts his left foot slightly forward of the right and points the toe of the right boot slightly away, in the anticipated direction of the target. The left-handed shooter will put his right foot forward, in mirror image.

Lead is dramatically affected by footwork. Proper footwork frees up the body, so when you start your swing, you are building speed at the muzzle. Muzzle speed allows you to swing though the target. Without proper footwork, the body binds up. The shoulders drop and the shooter is unable to keep his shoulders square with the target. *Keeping your shoulders square with the target is an essential element of stance.* If you have to take a step to square the body to the shot, the muzzle speed slows, and the target will beat you.

Proper Footwork

(Illustrated for a right-handed shooter)

Start with your feet in the position illustrated on page 43. The toe of your off-foot (back) comes to the arch of your shooting-foot (front.) As the bird rises, pivot so your shoulders are square with the flight path of the bird. The muzzle of the gun and your belly should be pointing in the same direction as your lead foot. Your weight is slightly forward on your lead foot, your hands and eyes are looking/ pointing at the target, and you are holding the muzzle just underneath your line of sight, at chin level. This enables you to point the muzzle of your gun on the bird as soon as you see it. This stance allows you to take the bird off your back foot or your front foot, depending on the flight path of the target.

The toe of your off-foot comes back to the arch of your shooting foot.

As the bird rises, pivot slightly on the forward foot and use the back "anchor" foot for balance and body control, as shown on page 45. This stance enables a shooter to pivot 180-degrees or more without having to reposition his feet. A stance that is wider than the width of the shoulders will restrict your movement. Begin pointing at the bird the moment you see it rise. There should be equal weight between your feet. As the bird continues to rise, start tracking the bird. Do not break or bend at the waist as you push your chin forward. Let your forehand naturally point the gun. Continue to pivot as you track the bird. Keep your shoulders and hips square with the flight path of the bird. Your focus should be entirely on the bird as you calculate your shot.

Continue to lean into the shot. Maintain your weight forward and keep your head steady as you bring the gun up to your cheek. When you mount

As the bird rises, pivot slightly on the forward foot.

Continue to lean into the shot. Maintain your weight
forward and keep your head steady.

your gun properly, you bring your gun to your cheek—you don't bring your head down to the gun. If your head is moving, your eyes are too, and you will not be able to accurately focus on—or track—the bird.

Moving and mounting the gun is one free-form action. With the Orvis method, the bird never beats the muzzle. The muzzle stays in contact with the bird the entire time. As the body is pivoting, the gun is being mounted.

Too often we see a shooter mount the gun before he focuses on the bird. This is incorrect. He must then attempt to catch up to the bird by tracking it over the barrels. If you see the bird and mount the gun immediately, before visually tracking its flight path, you then have to find the bird a second time. This involves two separate motions. Just remember, **proper gun mount is one, continuous motion.**

The Ready (or "Alert") Position

Each presentation begins with the ready, or "alert" position. You must come to the ready position before you mount the gun. This means your feet are in the proper position and your shoulders and hips squarely face the rising bird. The butt of the gun is tucked slightly under your arm. The muzzles are under the line of sight. Hunting with a good pointer or setter can buy you the important time you need to get into the ready position when the dog freezes on point. If your canine hunting companion is a flushing breed, you will know when he is "on" a bird. The ground he covers allows you to anticipate where a bird may flush. The wingshooter has little control over the hunting situation, but he does have control over his shot.

The Ready Position

The shooter prepares to take the ready position. He holds the stock firmly, but not in a stranglehold, with his shooting hand. His trigger finger rests alongside the trigger guard and his thumb is behind, not on, the safety.

The fingers of the pointing hand are spread out and do not come over the top of the barrels, so you do not impede your sight line across the rib. Maintain a firm but relaxed hold on the gun.

The proper way to pull a trigger is to bend the fleshy tip of your index finger at the first joint. If you wrap your finger around the trigger, you will pull it with your knuckle and this will jerk the trigger and throw off your shot.

PRESENTATION

THERE ARE THREE presentations in wingshooting: (1) The straight going-away shot; (2) the right-to-left crossing shot; and (3) the left-to-right crossing shot. The technique you use to shoot the straight going-away shot and the right-to-left crossing shot are similar. For the right-handed shooter, however, the left-to-right crossing shot is more difficult. Here, the full benefit of proper footwork comes into play. As you see in the pictorial sequence on the following pages, the shooter's stance allows her to track the target while pivoting 180-degrees. Gun mount is the same for all three presentations.

THE STRAIGHT GOING-AWAY SHOT

When the bird is sighted, the forehand and eyes point and track the bird.

The weight is on the forward foot.

The gun is flat and in contact with the target as it comes high into the cheek.

THE RIGHT-TO-LEFT CROSSING SHOT

Illustrated for the right-handed shooter

IDENTIFY YOUR TARGET, track the bird with your pointing hand and begin to mount the gun. Keep your legs straight. Your weight is equal between both feet, as shown in the illustration at right. The muzzle of the gun is below your line of sight. The safety is pushed off as you continue to visually track the bird. Bring the gun up to your cheek with minimal movement of your head. Keep your shoulders square with the rising bird as you continue to track the target. As you lean into the shot, your weight will move forward to the lead toe. The muzzle is still in contact with the target, and the lead hand is pointing at the bird. The gun slides forward. As you push the muzzle toward the bird, the trigger hand will come up to the cheek.

Track the bird with your pointing hand as you mount the gun.

As you swing with the bird, lean into the shot and continue to swing through the flight path. Pull the trigger without stopping your swing. You are not shooting the bird as much as the bird is flying into the shot. Keep your weight on the forward foot. Feel the right heel release off the ground. This frees you up so you can continue to pivot. Keep your weight forward on your front foot. Your back foot acts like a fulcrum. Your shoulders remain square to the target. Releasing the heel from the ground allows the swing to continue, even after the shot. This eliminates the need for lead perception.

Mount the gun as you continue to swing. Feel your left heel release off the ground as you lean into the shot.

Continue to track and swing through the bird. Remember, you are not shooting at the bird. The bird is flying into the shot.

Remember, as you swing, you pick up muzzle speed, which results in the allowance you need to swing through and past the flight path of the bird. Even when you think your shot has come in contact with the target, *keep swinging.* You never shoot at the bird. *The bird comes in contact with the shot.* Many variables determine an effective shot. The point of interception depends upon the speed of the bird in flight, distance, the size of the load, the type of shot (lead, steel, non-toxic shot, etc.) how the barrel is choked, gun gauge, and most importantly, you—the wingshooter.

THE LEFT-TO-RIGHT CROSSING SHOT

(Illustrated for a right-handed shooter)

This is the most difficult shot for the right-handed shooter. It allows the individual to take a shot off the right foot.

BEGIN AS BEFORE. Identify your target, track the bird with your pointing hand and begin to mount the gun. Keep your legs straight. Your weight is equal between both feet. The muzzle of the gun is below your line of sight. The safety is pushed off as you continue to visually track the bird as shown in the illustration at the right.

As the bird rises, bring the gun up and begin to track the bird. The muzzles must stay in contact with the bird. As you continue to track the bird, shift your weight to the right foot. Keep your shoulders over your right foot. In this presentation, it is correct to allow a slight arch in your back as you are going against your natural posture. Keep the weight from going beyond the front foot or you will have to shift your feet to avoid losing your balance and falling over, resulting in a missed shot. This sequence is illustrated on the next three pages.

As the bird rises, bring the gun up and begin to track the bird. As you continue to track the bird, shift your weight to the right foot.

Mount the gun as you continue to swing. Feel your left heel release off the ground as you lean into the shot.

Continue to track and swing through the bird. Remember, you are not shooting at the bird. The bird is flying into the shot.

Principles of
Wingshooting

Concentration

ONE OF THE MOST COMMON CAUSES of a missed shot—and the easiest to commit—is failing to maintain your concentration. Concentration, of course, depends on your ability to pay attention and to screen out everything around you except the target. Good concentration allows you to maintain a clear, crisp picture. To improve your concentration, find a detail on the leading edge of the target. By focusing on the leading edge, a good grouse hunter can see the crest, eye, beak, or the ruffs of the bird. A good quail hunter can tell if he is shooting a cock or a hen when he focuses on the head. Clays shooters can see the rings on the clay instead of a blur of orange. Concentrate on where the bird is going, not where it has been. The proper way to maintain your focus on the target is by keeping your head steady. If you fail to bring the gun to your cheek and instead bring your head down to the gun, you will miss. If your head is moving, your eyes are too.

Timing & Motion

Until you establish visual contact with the target, you are not ready to mount the gun.

Ease into the ready position as you track and point the target. Timing is dictated by the speed and flight path of the bird. We do not have control over the bird, but we do have control over the gun. Synchronize the muzzle speed of the gun with the speed of the target. The flight path of the bird dictates our movement. Just remember—the bird will not stop, so you shouldn't either.

LEAD

WHEN YOU FOLLOW-THROUGH THE TARGET, *lead happens*. Lead is not something you add onto the tail end of a shot. In the Orvis method, there is no predetermined forward allowance. It is part of the smooth, natural progression of the swing and follow-through beyond the point of impact. We are never hitting the birds; the birds run into the shot. If you follow the target and then add on what you think is the right lead, you will shoot behind the target. This is because you have stopped, looked at your gun, and attempted to judge the distance. The calculation you make to establish forward allowance happens as you see the bird rise and track its flight path when you lock your eyes on the target. Experience in different shooting situations will help you judge the speed and path of the target and determine the amount of follow through you will need.

The Orvis method allows the shooter to adapt to most shooting conditions and adjust to the wiles and eccentricities of the birds that he is hunting. Forward allowance is the product of good footwork, proper form, and effective follow-through.

Eye Dominance

Just as we favor our right or our left hand, we also unconsciously favor our right or our left eye. The eye that we favor is called the dominant eye. Our dominant eye does not necessarily focus more clearly than the other eye. It simply means that it relays visual stimuli to the brain faster than the other eye—approximately 14 milliseconds faster, to be exact.

If the dominant eye is on the same side of the body as your dominant hand, you should have no problem with the way you focus on the target. However, if you are right-handed and your left eye is dominant (or left-handed and right-eye dominant), then you have a condition known as *cross dominance*. If a person mounts the gun to the right side of his face while the left eye controls his visual perception, he will shoot to the left of the target. If your vision fails to align with the rib of the barrel, your dominant eye will have to be corrected.

There are three choices available to a shooter with cross dominance. (1) He can learn to shoot from the other shoulder; (2) He can close his dominant eye as he tracks the bird; (3) He can put a piece of opaque tape or smear some lip balm on the lens of the shooting glasses over his dominant eye. You need to block the theoretical straight line that is between the pupil of the eye and the barrel bead at the muzzle. Do not block out the entire field of vision. You just need to interrupt or slow the speed of visual perception so that the eye over the barrels can compensate. Experiment with each of these three options to determine what works best for you.

The best option for a wingshooter is to close the off-dominant eye as he tracks the bird. This gives accurate visual control over the shooting field. In sporting clays, blocking out the lens with tape or lip balm works well because the shooter is in a controlled shooting environment. Whatever you do, just remember: your eyes control the way you shoot.

SAFE CARRY POSITION

ASSUME A SAFE CARRY POSITION when you walk into the hunting area. Your gun should be fully unloaded. Load your gun only when you perceive a potentially promising hunting situation. Close the gun smartly. Check that your safety is on and be sure your finger is not on the trigger. Control the muzzle of your gun.

SAFE SHOOTING ZONES

WHEN YOU ARE HUNTING with one or more people, it is important that you establish a safe shooting zone before you enter the field.

The first and foremost rule of hunting is to be certain of your shot. It is far wiser to surrender a shot if you are uncertain where your hunting partners, guides, and gun dogs are than to run the risk of injuring someone. Regularly communicate with your hunting partner. Establish a language you both understand. Follow these rules:

1. *Everyone should be clear about what is expected of one another.* Whether you are crossing a cornfield,

straddling a hedgerow, or attempting to walk through thick cover in the woods, you must know where others are at all times. Stay a safe visual distance apart and maintain the line. This distance depends on the hunting situation. If there is any variation to the designated drive, arrange in advance a signal or call so the others know what you want. You should always be well within calling distance of your partners. Communicate almost continuously with your partner when in thick cover.

2. *If you are hunting with one other person, the hunter on the left should point his gun to the left or ahead of him, never to the right.* The hunter on the right should point his gun to his right or ahead of him, never to the left. If there are three at hand,

the hunter in the middle should point his gun ahead of him, not to the left or right. Never carry a break-open gun closed over your shoulder with the muzzle pointing behind you. If someone is behind you or you make a sudden turn, you may find yourself in a potentially unsafe hunting situation.

3. *Never shoot across or behind your hunting partner.* You will subject him to muzzle blast—or worse.

4. *Never run ahead of the line.* If you do, you may fall in the line of fire and force your partner to sacrifice his shot. This will create bad feelings and can ruin the hunt.

5. *Do not lag behind your partner.* You are not shooting within your safety zone otherwise. If a crossover shot comes within your zone, you should not attempt to take it. You will be shooting behind your partner—and that is unsafe.

6. *The most effective range of a shotgun is under 50 yards; however, the possible range of a fired cartridge can exceed 600 yards.* Never assume that anything outside of 50 yards is within safe range. If you can see a person, dog, or an unidentifiable object outside of 50 yards, surrender the shot. Assume that anything you are able to see is going to be within effective range of a discharged gun.

7. *Observe Hunter's Safety Rules.*

CHOKE

CHOKE IS THE DEGREE OF CONSTRICTION at the muzzle of a barrel. There are five basic degrees of choke: Cylinder (C), Improved Cylinder or quarter-choke (IC), Modified or half-choke (M), Improved Modified or three-quarter choke (IM), or Full (F).

Cylinder

A bore without any constriction at the muzzle is virtually a straight tube and therefore has no choke. Cylinder is best for short-range shooting in thick cover and other places were the widest possible spread is most efficient.

Improved Cylinder

There is a slight constriction at the muzzle of a barrel choked IC. This narrows the spread, steadies the pellets, and creates a tighter, more consistent pattern.

Modified

Modified is a general-purpose choke that has slightly more constriction at the muzzle than IC and therefore creates a tighter pattern than is effective at 40 yards. Usually the left barrel of a side-by-side game gun is choked modified if the right is choked IC, allowing the second shot to spread effectively a further 15 yards than the first, as the target distances itself from the shooter.

Improved Modified

Seen on British and continental guns, but rarely on American-made guns, IM is effective for shots taken at 40-50 yards, such as those encountered with driven birds.

Full

The maximum constriction at the muzzle is a barrel choked full, which is optimum for shots over 30 or 35 yards.

About the Orvis Shooting Schools

Orvis Manchester

ORVIS MANCHESTER IS LOCATED in historic Manchester, Vermont, one of New England's most picturesque villages. It is here in New England that the target game of sporting clays was first invented. Sporting clays mimic the flight patterns of wild birds. The game was invented in England; however, Orvis holds the distinction of bringing sporting clays to the United States. The stations at Orvis Manchester have been set up to simulate a wide variety of typical field shots, including upland-type going away and crossing shots, high incoming and driven-style presentations, and dove and waterfowl pass shooting situations. Clays mimicking springing teal and quail challenge the shooter from both sides of a tote road. Shooting instruction in this kind of controlled environment allows the student to better understand wingshooting. The Manchester school is limited to sixteen shooters with a maximum student-to-instructor ratio of 4:1. Two- or three-day programs are offered from mid-July through mid-October.

Orvis Mays Pond

Orvis May's Pond Plantation is a 6,000 acre Southern plantation located in the Florida panhandle, approximately 45 minutes east of Tallahassee. Shooting schools are offered in the late fall and winter. Early Bird Schools are conducted in August and September particularly for those who want to practice for dove season. For this reason, particular interest is placed on pass shooting, as well as waterfowl and quail hunting situations. The classroom is a restored one-room Georgia schoolhouse where lunches are catered each day. Students stay in Thomasville, Georgia, about 20 minutes from the plantation.

Orvis Sandanoma

Orvis Sandanona is located in the historic Hudson River Valley in picturesque Millbrook, New York. Sandanona is the oldest licensed hunting preserve in the country, dating back to the 19th century when it was a private shooting club. The 300-acre shooting grounds, home of one of the most challenging sporting clays courses in the world, is only 60 miles north of New York City, yet the atmosphere is rustic and reminiscent of a bygone era. Sandanona is open year-round. One- or two-day shooting schools are available.

All Orvis Shooting Schools include comprehensive instruction by professionally trained shooting instructors, lunch each day of class, all targets and cartridges, use of a double gun, eye and ear protection, recoil shields if needed, and a professional custom gun fitting and consultation.

ABOUT THE SERIES EDITOR

LAURIE MORROW is the editor of the *Orvis Field Guide Series*, as well as author of a half-dozen books on fishing and shotgunning, including *Shooting Sports for Women*, *The Italian Gun* (with Steve Smith), *The Woman Angler* and *Cold Noses & Warm Hearts,* a Literary Guild Selection published by Willow Creek Press. She is a contributor to *Sports Afield, Field & Stream, Outdoor Life, Petersen's Shotguns, The Retriever Journal, Pointing Dog Journal* and *Shooting Sportsman* and is the adventure travel journalist for Volvo Cars of North America.

Photo: Ned Bullock